Thank you to the generous team who gave their time and talents to make this book possible:

Authors
Carol Settgast and Jane Kurtz

Illustrators
Carol Settgast and students
from Sheridan Elementary School

Creative directors
Caroline Kurtz, Jane Kurtz,
Elizabeth Spor Taylor, and Kenny Rasmussen

Translator
Asmaa Ahmed

Editors
Mastewal Abera and
Woubeshet Ayenew

Designer
Beth Crow

Ready Set Go Books, an Open Hearts Big Dreams Project

The Journey of Butterflies

رحلة الفراشات

English and Arabic

A long, long journey begins
with one flap of the wings.

رحلة طويلة جدًا تبدأ برفرفة
واحدة من الأجنحة.

Flap!
رفرفي!
Flap!
رفرفي!
Flap!
رفرفي!

At Gullele Botanical Garden, scientists study plants and butterflies that are important to Ethiopia.

في حديقة جوليلي للنباتات، يدرس العلماء النباتات والفراشات التي تعتبر مهمة جدًا لأثيوبيا.

A female Painted Lady Butterfly perches on a flower.
This species of butterfly is beautifully colored with
orange, brown, black, and white markings.

تهبط فراشة ملونة على الزهرة. هذا النوع من
الفراشات جميل وملون بالألوان البرتقالي والبني
والأسود والعلامات البيضاء.

The butterfly searches for a thistle plant
to lay her many eggs one by one.

تبحث الفراشة عن نبات ذي أشواك لتضع
بيضاتها، واحدة تلو الأخرى.

Look!
أنظر!

Look!
أنظر!

Look!
أنظر!

Five days later, a Painted Lady
Butterfly larva—about as big as a grain
of rice--breaks out of its soft shell.

بعد خمسة أيام، انفصلت يرقة فراشة
ملونة، في حجم حبة الأرز، وخرجت من
شرنقتها الناعمة.

What is the first thing it eats
to make its body strong?

ما أول شيء تأكله ليكون جسمها قويًا؟

Its own eggshell.

قشرة يرقتها نفسها.

It grows into a caterpillar with strong jaws that chew from side to side instead of up and down the way people chew.

تبدأ في النمو لتكون دودة بفِكين قويين يمضغان من جانب لجانب بدلًا من الحركة من أعلى لأسفل كما يمضغ الناس.

The caterpillar's job is to eat and grow to get strong for the journey ahead. It weaves a silk tent to hide from enemies -or predators- that may want to eat it. Under the tent, the caterpillar is safe to eat as many leaves as it can.

وظيفة الدودة هي أن تأكل وتكبر وتكون قوية للرحلة أمامها. تقوم بنسج خيمة من الحرير للاختباء من الأعداء — أو المفترسين — الذين قد يريدون أن يأكلونها. تحت الخيمة، الدودة آمنة ويمكنها أن تأكل أوراق شجر بقدر ما تستطيع.

As the caterpillar grows bigger, it sheds its skin 4 times.

بينما تتنمو الدودة وتكبر، تغير جلدها ٤ مرات.

Grow!

أكبري!

Grow!

أكبري!

Grow!

أكبري!

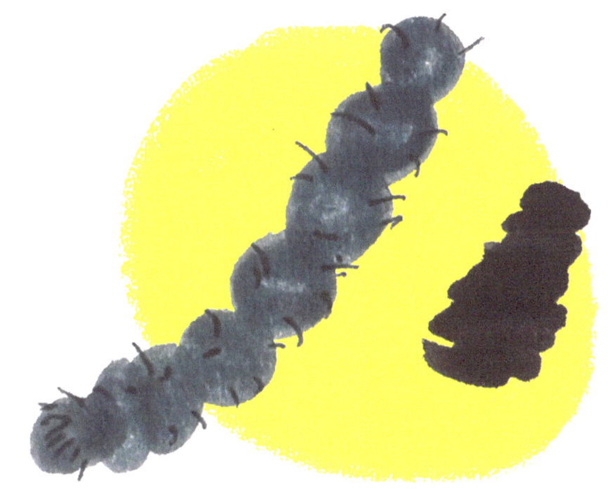

Soon, it's time for more changes. The Painted Lady caterpillar weaves a silk knot. It hangs down in the shape of a hook.

سريعًا، يحين وقت المزيد من التغيير. تنسج دودة الفراشة الملونة عقدة حريرية. تتعلق من لأسفل في شكل خطاف.

The skin of the caterpillar becomes a hard case.
Inside that case, a very different body grows.

يصبح جلد الدودة كحافظة صلبة. داخل الحافظة،
ينمو جسم مختلف تمامًا.

Wait!　　　　**Wait!**　　　　**Wait!**

انتظري!　　　　انتظري!　　　　انتظري!

A week later,
a Painted Lady
butterfly crawls out of
the case. The caterpillar
has been transformed!
It waves its wings to dry
them for the next part of
its life...the first flight!

بعد أسبوع، تزحف فراشة
ملونة من الحافظة. لقد
تحولت الدودة! تقوم
برفرفة جناحها لتجففهم
للجزء التالي من حياتها ...
رحلة الطيران الأولى!

This is how angels must feel!

هكذا يكون شعور الملائكة بالتأكيد!

The butterflies need to get ready for an important and difficult journey called migration. During Ethiopia's dry season, flowers disappear, so the butterflies must fly north. They build up body fat for the trip by drinking nectar.

تحتاج الفراشات أن تستعد لرحلة مهمة وصعبة تسمى الهجرة. أثناء موسم الجفاف الأثيوبي، تختفي الزهور، لذلك يجب أن تطير الفراشات تجاه الشمال. تقوم بتخزين الدهون في جسمها بشرب الرحيق من أجل الرحلة.

Butterflies can't read
a compass the way
explorers sometimes do.
لا تستطيع الفراشات قراءة
البوصلة كما يفعل
المستكشفين أحيانًا.

But butterflies can use the sun as a
compass. Luckily, Ethiopia is known for
having thirteen months of sunshine.

لكن الفراشات تستطيع استخدام الشمس كبوصلة.
لحسن الحظ، أثيوبيا معروفة بسطوع الشمس لمدة
ثلاثة عشر شهر في السنة.

Painted Lady Butterflies can travel up to 160 kilometers in a day. Sometimes the butterflies fly high in the sky over Ethiopia's northern mountains and Abay Falls.

تستطيع الفراشات الملونة السفر لمسافة ١٦٠ كيلومتر في اليوم. أحيانًا تطير الفراشات عاليًا في السماء فوق جبال أثيوبيا الشمالية وشلالات آبي.

Other times, the butterflies fly low to the ground. Here, they search for nectar from the flowers in the ancient city of Gondar.

في أوقات أخرى، تطير الفراشات قريبًا من الأرض. هنا، تكون تبحث عن رحيق الأزهار في مدينة جوندار القديمة.

Low!
أسفل**!**

Low!
أسفل**!**

Low!
أسفل**!**

As the butterflies cross the Sahara Desert on their way north towards Egypt, they get help from wind currents that push them across the sky.

بينما تعبر الفراشات الصحراء الكبرى في طريقها شمالًا نحو مصر، تساعدها تيارات الهواء التي تدفعها لتطير في السماء.

Sometimes, they must fly for 24 hours
without stopping.

أحيانًا، يكون عليها أن تطير لمدة
٢٤ ساعة بدون توقف.

How do the butterflies know where to go?
Their eyes and their brains give them
information.

كيف تعرف الفراشات أين تذهب؟
تعطيها عيونها وعقلها المعلومات.

Some of the butterflies fly
over Egyptian pyramids.

بعض الفراشات تطير
فوق أهرامات مصر.

Their wings get tired, but they don't stop.

تتعب أجنحتها، لكنها لا تتوقف.

The journey takes them across the
Mediterranean Sea.

تأخذها الرحلة عبر البحر
المتوسط.

They can't stop until they
reach a place with enough
rain so plants can grow.

لا يمكنها التوقف حتى تصل
إلى مكان به مطر كافي حيث
تستطيع النباتات النمو.

They land on the Greek island of Crete.

تهبط على جزيرة كريت اليونانية.

Goodnight little butterfly! Soon
it will be time for the next part of
the journey to begin.

تصبحين على خير أيتها الفراشة
الصغيرة! سريعًا يكون وقت بدء
الجزء التالي من الرحلة.

Sleep!
نامي!
Sleep!
نامي!
Sleep!
نامي!

The Painted Lady butterfly looks for thistle plants so she can lay eggs that will turn into caterpillars that will turn into butterflies.

تبحث الفراشة الملونة عن نباتات ذات أشواك حتى يمكنها وضع بيضاتها، التي ستتحول لدودة ثم تتحول لفراشة.

These new butterflies will continue a journey
further into Europe. More butterflies will be born.
When weather turns cold in Europe, there will
be Painted Lady butterflies with strong wings to
flap, ready to fly back to Ethiopia.

هذه الفراشات الجديدة سوف تستكمل الرحلة أكثر
داخل أوروبا. سوف تولد المزيد من الفراشات.
عندما يصبح الطقس أكثر برودة في أوروبا،
ستكون هناك فراشات ملونة
بأجنحة قوية
ترفرف بها،
ويكون جاهزة
للعودة طائرة
لأثيوبيا.

About the Story

In 2009, scientists in the United Kingdom set up a citizen science project where ordinary people could help unlock the mystery of where U.K. painted lady butterflies went every autumn. The answer was an amazing 9,000-mile round trip journey from Africa to the Arctic Circle, the longest insect migration journey ever discovered. This Ready Set Go (RSG) book also had a long journey to reach publication. Many people helped to research, write, illustrate, and translate it. Many others will print and distribute this book to children in Ethiopia and around the world. Many of those children will be inspired to plant more flowers that butterflies need to be able to survive.

The Project Manager for **The Journey of Butterflies**, Carol Settgast, met Jane Kurtz and other Ethiopia Reads volunteers in Ethiopia in 2010, during a cultural trip for educators. Carol has volunteered with Ethiopia Reads ever since. (The Ethiopia Reads Ethiopian staff will work with Carol on planning science and reading events, using this book to help Ethiopian children grow their understand of butterfly life.) While Carol was the librarian at Sheridan Elementary School in Junction City, Kansas, she helped students write Help! one of the first Ready Set Go Books. In 2021, Jane Kurtz did an author visit at Sheridan Elementary School and this new book began its long journey supported by many people—just as The Journey of Butterflies shows a long migration that can take about six generations of individual insects.

In order for this book to reach its destination into the hands of children, the authors must also thank Elizabeth Spor Taylor for helping with the vision for each page and also the Entomological Society of America for a Chrysalis Fund Grant that will support the Open Hearts Big Dreams printing of this book in Ethiopia. We couldn't have done this project without you!

Dedicated to Rich Male who models how to stretch our wings and fly.

About the Authors and Illustrators

Thank you to the generous team who gave their time and talents to make this butterfly book possible.

Sheridan Elementary School Researchers:
- Sheridan Librarian – Heather Ryan...Lead Instructor for Painted Lady Butterfly individual research projects in 5th grade
- Mrs. Martino – 5th grade Teacher and Students
- Mrs. Schlagel – 5th grade Teacher and Students
- Mrs. Pederson and Mrs. Steward– 2nd grade Teachers and their Students who conducted actual field studies by raising Painted Lady butterflies in classrooms and releasing them to the wild.

International Entomologists: Abeje Kassie, Dr. Gregory Zolnerowich, Dr. Gerard Talavera, Dr. Constanti Stefanescu helped answer research questions from Sheridan 5th graders for individual research projects.

Writing Team:
- Project Coach: Jane Kurtz with Elizabeth Spor Taylor
- Project Manager: Carol Settgast
- Principal Dorothy Coleman, Lead Instructor in Writer's Workshop for 5th graders creating individual research projects which built the scientific foundation for this book

Illustration Team:
Sheridan Art Teacher – Rebekah Thomas, instructing ALL Sheridan students K – 5th grade on creating illustrations of the butterfly life cycle used in this book

Artistic Creative Team: Carol Settgast, Elizabeth Spor Taylor, Beth Crow

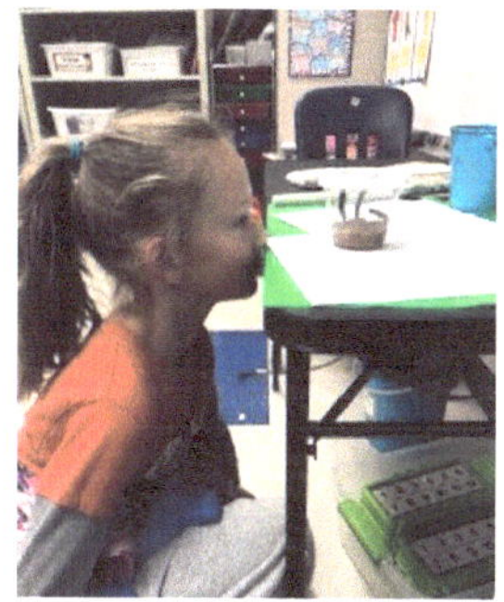

About Open Hearts Big Dreams

Open Hearts Big Dreams Fund (OHBD) was founded by Ellenore Angelidis, inspired by her Ethiopian born daughter, Leyla Marie Fasika; both are key volunteers. OHBD is a United State 501(c)(3) not-for-profit organization that believes the chance to dream big dreams should not depend on where in the world you are born. Our mission is "Inspiring and empowering youth (K-14) to reimagine their futures by providing literacy, STEAM, and leadership opportunities."

OHBD harnesses the power of collaboration. We are made up of a small number of part-time paid staff and a large number of highly motivated volunteers with advanced skills, including artistic, editorial, translation, and high-tech expertise in Ethiopia, the Diaspora and globally. Our culture of innovation means we act fast on new ideas. Since 2017, we've produced more than 1000 bilingual, culturally appropriate early reader titles and a number of STEM and Model programs to increase literacy, inclusion, and leadership.

In Ethiopia, for Ethiopia; OHBD is based in the U.S. but we are committed to working with local content creators and to producing quality books in Ethiopia. Local opportunities and production builds local knowledge and capacity.

About OHBD Ready Set Go Books

Reading has the power to change lives, but many children and adults in Ethiopia cannot read. One reason is that Ethiopia doesn't have enough books in local languages to give people a chance to practice reading. Ready Set Go books wants to close that gap and open a world of ideas and possibilities for kids and their communities.

When you buy an OHBD-RSG book, you provide critical funding to create and distribute more books.

Learn more at: http://openheartsbigdreams.org/book-project/ or find all our books at: https://ohbd-rsgbooks.com

OHBD Proudly Prints in Ethiopia

OHBD developed our own local printing capacity and have a number of our books available to pick up in Addis. They are available for bulk purchase and we regularly donate to schools, libraries and local organizations serving kids. Please contact us at ellenore@openheartsbigdreams.org if interested in samples or ordering.

So far, we have printed and distributed (with collaborating organizations) hundreds of thousands of copies of our books in numerous languages in country.

Our goal is to get these books to all elementary students across Ethiopia.

About the Language

Arabic (العربية, al-'arabiyyah) is a Semitic language and a root language. The Arabic language is written from right to left in a consonant alphabet, which is also called an abjad.

Millions of people speak it as their first language and many more people understand it as a second language. Although many of the countries that use Arabic as their official language are in the Middle East, Arabic is also the most widely spoken language on the continent of Africa. Arabic speakers in Africa account for more than half of the total Arabic speakers in the world. It is recognized as the official language in countries in North and Sib-Saharan Africa including Egypt, Libya, Morocco, Mauritania, Eritrea, and Algeria. Arabic is a co-official language in some countries such as Chad, Djibouti, and Somalia, and is also widely spoken in countries that do not recognize it as a national language.

Since it is so widely spoken throughout the world, Arabic is one of the official languages of the United Nations.

About the Translation

Ellenore Angelidis, the founder of Open Hearts Big Dreams (OHBD), was a long time Director at Amazon in both legal and business roles. She reached out to former colleagues on the Amazon Global Legal Team for advice and assistance when ReadySetGo Books was ready to expand into Arabic, a frequently spoken language in a number of African countries. The Kindle Books group at Amazon generously offered to cover the cost of translation. More than 100 of OHBD's early readers were translated into Arabic as part of Amazon's on-going corporate commitment to support literacy and to create more reading opportunities globally. These books will be used for literacy and education efforts in Arabic-speaking countries in Africa as well as for language and culture preservation efforts globally.

100+ unique OHBD-RSG books available in over 20 languages!

  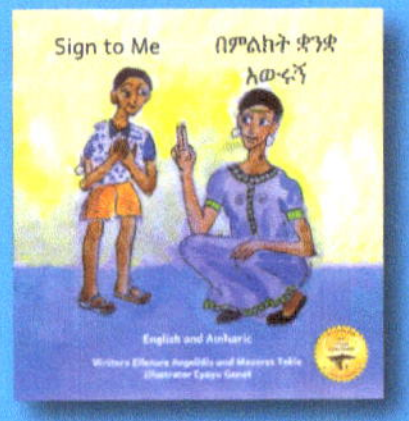  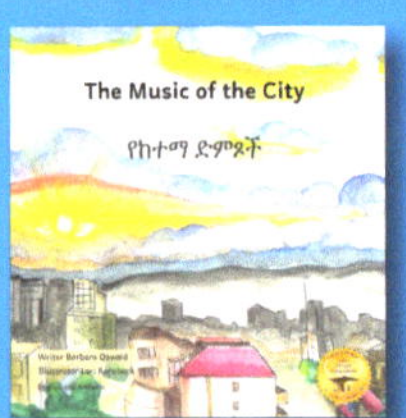 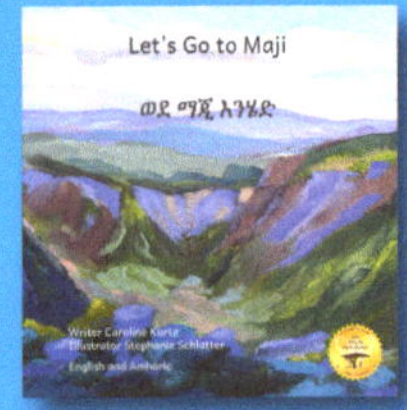

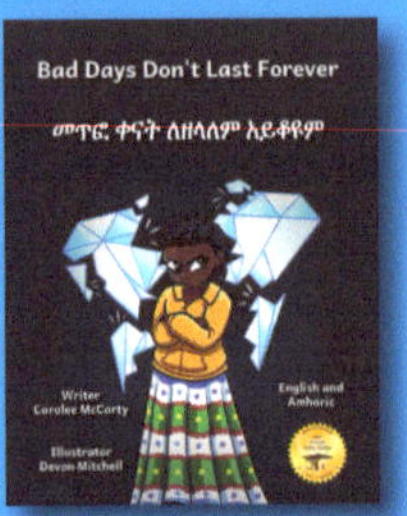 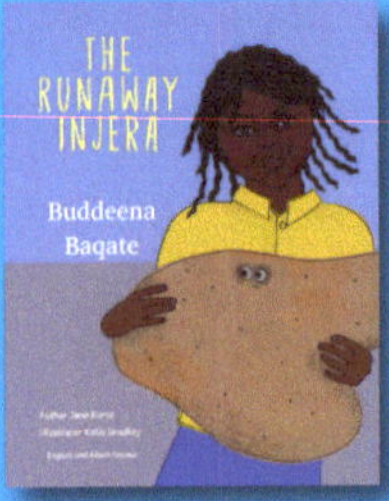 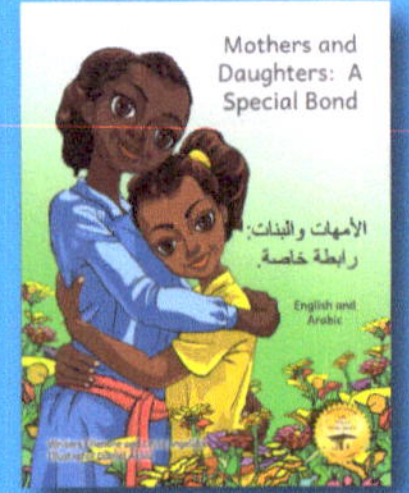   

  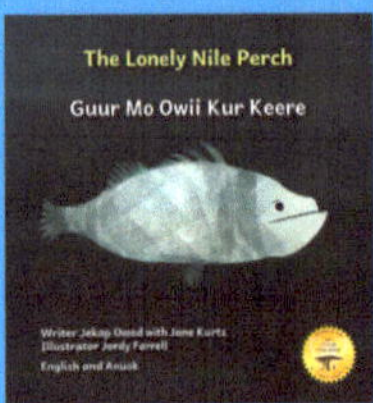 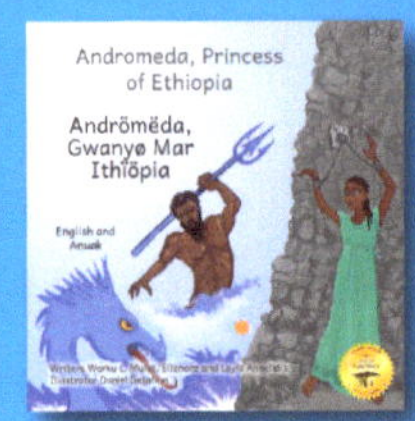  

To view all available titles, go to https://ohbd-rsgbooks.com/shop or scan QR code

Open Heart Big Dreams is pleased to offer discounts for bulk orders, educators and organizations.

Contact ellenore@openheartsbigdreams.org for more information.